FROM HOPE
ST ALBAI
DORSET DEVO]

ISBN: 0-907683-11-8

I would like to thank Mr D. Feasey who provided me with much information on local wrecks, and taught me how to hold my breath for an hour underwater! The Lyme Regis and Bridport Museum and the Greenwich Maritime Museum, also Penny Jones, the next best thing to Tippex. The drawings in this booklet are by Trevor Price and the words and mistakes by me.

By Nigel J. Clarke
Drawings by Trevor Price.
Printed by C. J. Creed, Broadoak, Bridport, Dorset.
Photographs courtesy of Weymouth Museum.
Published by

N. J. Clarke Publications
Tollgate Cottage
Tappers Knapp
Uplyme
Lyme Regis
Dorset

Telephone: Lyme Regis 02924 3669

*"GERTRUDE", wrecked on 26th August, 1894.
On the rocks at Portland.*

*"MADELEINE TRISTAN", wrecked 20th September, 1930
Chesil Cove, Portland.*

INTRODUCTION
"FROM HOPES NOSE TO SAINT ALBANS HEAD"

The sea and shoreline of East Devon and West Dorset have claimed many vessels with countless lives lost. Both Dorset and Devon have a traditional maritime history of fishing, commerce, smuggling and in recent years pleasure boating. The coastline from St. Albans Head to Hope's Nose has few sheltered places. The granite arm of Portland Bill has protected many ships from the worst of the prevailing south west winds, but has also claimed many trying to round the Bill. Many vessels have met their doom on the ledges of Kimmeridge, but the worst stretch of the coastline is the Chesil Beach, a long finger of pebble and stone running from West Bay to Portland, steep and graded by the sea. The small pebbles are at the western end of the beach and rocks and large stones to the east. A vessel caught in Lyme Bay during a storm has few places to seek shelter. Many were blown towards the desolation and wreck on the Chesil. The dead often buried in communal graves. The age of the engine has lessened the casulties along the coast, as man is no longer dependent on the wind to move across the oceans. The ships have become larger and no longer come close inshore. The volume of trade is much reduced to the small coastal ports, but in recent years losses of pleasure-craft have increased though not with the fatalities of the nineteenth century, due to the diligence of the rescue services.

An estimation of wrecks along the Dorset and Devon coast is difficult; records, positions and names are often confused. There is little doubt that more ships were sunk off Axmouth (near Seaton) than are recorded. At one time Axmouth was an important Roman port, till during the Dark ages the river mouth silted and became blocked. Little if any visible trace of these early wrecks remain.

The range of wrecks along the coastline is staggering, submarines, landing craft, a mud hopper, dredger, trawlers, merchantman, and even treasure ship smashed onto the Chesil, carrying gold bullion. There have also been two balloons, lost in Lyme Bay, one carrying a member of Parliament. On Portland the wrecks were sometimes induced by the local population to crash onto the rocks, the stranded vessels stripped. The bounty from the sea helped islanders survive on a barren and windswept rocky outcrop, that protrudes into the English Channel. Further to the west at Exmouth, there is a treacherous sand bar, called Pole Sands. In the last two hundred years some twenty-eight vessels have been wrecked on it, and countless more in earlier centuries.

I hope you find this booklet interesting as it reveals the stories behind some of the wrecks that occured between Hopes Nose and St. Alban's Head.

Nigel J. Clarke

THE FORMIDABLE   START POINT
1st JANUARY 1915
(15.000 tons)

The sinking of the Formidable was a major disaster for the Navy and a tragic loss of men. Admiral Bayly was the new commander of the Fifth Battle Squadron, having transfered from the Northern Fleet, where he had been in charge of a dreadnought battleship. He was very much a man of the old school and under-estimated the power of submarine warfare. Shortly before Christmas he received permission to take the squadron from Nore (in Essex) to Portland, off which he was to train and excercise. He sailed down the Channel with an escort of 6 destroyers, which returned to Nore after reaching Folkstone. For the remaining journey, to Portland, there was to be no protective screen, apart from the light cruisers HMS Topaz and HMS Diamond. The Admiral arrived off Portland with his squadron at daybreak, on the 31st of December. The training and firing exercise in Lyme Bay lasted all day. At dusk, the Admiral decided against putting into Portland Harbour, and remained at sea (there had been no reported German submarine activity in the area), to restart the exercise in the morning. The squadron proceeded to stem east towards the Isle of Wight. Shortly after dark the course was changed to west (this was in accordance with naval regulations, to forstall attack by Submarine). The night was clear, with good visability and a bright moon. The ships kept a straight course, the two light cruisers to the front and the Formidable to the rear.

Unknown to Admiral Bayly, all the previous afternoon, a German submarine had observed the excercise and had stalked the squadron, awaiting a chance for a shot at the Formidable. Even the abrupt change of course, at dusk was pointless, with the moon silhouetting the outline of the warships clearly. At 2.30 a.m., as the squadron drew near to Start Point, off the Devon coast, the patient submarine fired its torpedo, striking the Formidable, in the starboard side and knocking out the engine, the ship soon listed 20° The weather was deteriorating. The position of the ship was hopeless, as she foundered in the swell, disabled with no steerage. It was decided to start evacuating the ship. The ships pinnace, launch and two boats were filled with sailors. One of the boats capsized, in the swell. The light cruiser, HMS Topaz came alongside and succeeded in taking off 43 men, in difficult conditions. An hour passed, when a second torpedo struck the Formidable, this time on the portside, the ship swung up onto an even keel, as the sea rushed into the gaping hole. Water logged, with no engine power the crew were unable to launch the rest of the safety boats. There was no panic and discipline remained at all times, dispite the grave situation of the battleship. The Topaz tried to fetch a passing liner, but with no success. HMS Diamond (the other light cruiser) was ordered to stand-off from the Formidable, due to the danger of another torpedo attack. The order was given to abandon ship at 4.45, two and a half hours after the first torpedo hit the ship. As the sea and the wind rose the crew scrambled over the side, into the freezing January water. The ship went down bow first, her screws and rudder standing clear of the water, she then sank completely. The Formidable launch was picked up by the Brixam trawler 'Provident'! The launch was overcrowded and nearly sinking. The Provident was able to come alongside and took off 71 sailors. Another Formidable boat was found on the beach at Abbotsbury, empty and upside down. More fortunate was the boat that landed in

H.M.S. "FORMIDABLE"

thick fog at Lyme Regis, though some had died of exposure. The survivers and bodies were taken into the Pilot Boat, where one man though to be dead was revived by the licking of the landlords dog, Lassie.

Out of a total crew of 780, only 233 survived. At the subsequent inquiry Admiral Bayly was relieved of his command, though little of it was now left, and given a shore posting as President of the Royal Naval College Greenwich. Later in the war he was to serve with distinction as head of operations at the South of Ireland station.

GALICIA SUNK BY TORPEDO

GALICIA   12th MAY 1917   TEIGNMOUTH
Typical of the many first world war wrecks in the area is that of the S.S.Galicia. She was an armed merchantman of 5,922 tons. On the 12th of May, 1917 she struck a sea mine and started to sink, 3 miles east of Teignmouth. The Galicia was in ballast though on board were 59 passengers and crew, who were rescued by the Teignmouth lifeboat, a tug and a naval auxillary vessel. The vessel is still visable on the sea bed, though broken up. At the time of sinking she was owned by the Pacific Steam Navigation Company.

S. S. BRETAGNE (14,399 tons) sunk after collision in 1918, off Exmouth.

PILOTS BLAMED FOR NEGLEGENCE
AT EXMOUTH

FRIENDS   **DAWLISH-EXMOUTH**
27th AUGUST 1933

The Friends was a 73 ton schooner, one of the many that carried coal to the south from the northern coalfield. On the 3rd of January 1854 the Friends arrived off Exmouth, anchored and waited for the pilot to come out to guide the schooner up through the hazardous entrance and sand bar of the river Exe. The flares were burnt, to notify the pilots that their assistance was required. All the time the Friends waited the weather deteriorated. In no time, the wind had increased to storm force ten, and still no pilots. In desperation, the captain of the Friends weighed anchor and attempted to seek shelter further along the coast, at Torbay. The south west wind held him close to the shore, and the ship eventually ran into the rocks, to the west of Exmouth. Luckly, the crew were able to scramble ashore, but the ship was wrecked. A subsequent inquiry cleared the Exmouth pilots of neglegence,

18,000 FISH LOST OVERBOARD

JOHN 1573   **EXMOUTH**

The John is not a spectacular wreck, but is one of the few early wrecks who's fate we know about, because of the inquiry its sinking subsequently brought. The John was a mother ship to a fishing fleet, which had been working successfully off the Newfoundland coast. She arrived off Exmouth and awaited the pilot to guide her up stream, to unload her catch of fish. The pilot engaged was John Parsons, his knowledge of the river would seem to be wanting, for instead of piloting the ship to its berth, his course set it on the sand bank at the entrance of the river. Of the

70,000 fish carried by the vessel, 18,000 were lost and the ship was so severley damaged that she was eventually broken up. The owner sued the pilot for negligence and compensation of nearly £300.

LIFEBOAT CRITICIZED

JULIA   1867   EXMOUTH

It is rare for a failed rescue attempt to bring criticism on the would-be rescuers, but in the case of the wrecking of the Julia, the Lifeboat of the day received a proportion of the blame. The Julia was an Exeter owned brigantine carrying a cargo of coal. She arrive off Exmouth on the 5th of January 1867. The brigantine attempted to enter the river, in difficult conditions, as there was a south eastern gale blowing. The Julia was blown onto Pole Sands, which stradles the entrance to the Exe. Many saw her trouble, as she lay on the sands, buffeted by large waves. The lifeboat, kept opposite the sand bar was late in reacting, as there was trouble finding the coxswain. When at last the lifeboat was launched she was pushed away down stream by the wind and tide. Some local fishermen manned a revenue pinnace and were able to row against the wind and tide, though too late. The Julia had broken up, the only man that the fishermen were able to rescue was a Scottish Sailor, the rest of the crew were drowned.

After the tragic incident there was much criticism of the lifeboats slow reaction time and its inability to row against the tide and wind. Though there was no official reprimand the inquiry did find that the Julia was unfit to put to sea. It was a sad affair, made worse because everyone could see the event from the shore but could do nothing.

10

'THE DUCHESS' STRANDED ON SIDMOUTH BEACH

DUCHESS OF DEVONSHIRE

27th AUGUST 1933   SIDMOUTH

(excursion Steamer)

The Duchess of Devonshire was a small excursion steamer, that sailed between Torquay and Seaton. She had been bought from the Devon Dock and Steamship Company who no longer found her economic to run. The new owners were able to resume boat trips along the coast. It was common practice to land the passengers on the beaches of Seaton and Sidmouth, by driving the bow up, onto the beach. On 27th of August, 1933, Captain Colebard steamed ahead, onto the beach of Sidmouth, to let his forty passengers disembark and stroll round the pleasant Devon resort. As he manouvered onto the beach, a large wave hit The Duchess, on her port, pushing the steamer, broadside onto the beach, where she unfortunately landed on top of some concrete staging. Unable to reverse off the beach the Captain decided to wait for the next tide. As the tide went out the concrete staging holed the stricken steamer. This was soon repaired, and the ship pumped out. At the next high tide the vessel still refused to budge, after several more desperate attempts it was decided to break the ship for scrap. Plates and parts are still occasionally found on the beach, especially after a storm.

SIX RATER WRECKED AT LYME

HMS SOLEBAY   1709   LYME REGIS

HMS Solebay is one of the few recorded warships lost near Lyme Regis. She was a six rater (had six guns). She was sunk in a storm, and smashed onto the rocks, probably to the east of the town, between Church Cliffs and Black Venn. In recent years some old cannons have been found by divers in this area.

TOWNFOLK RESCUE SPANISH CREW
LAGUITUS DE LILLE DIEU 1748 LYME REGIS
(Spanish Trader)

The Laguitus was carrying a cargo of wool, which may have come from Lyme Regis, which at this time was nearing the end of its life as a port for the trading of wool, the harbour being to small for the larger vessels. The Laguitus was caught in a southwest gale and drifted in the rough sea past the town onto the ledges and cliffs to the east. Townsfolk seeing the difficulty were able to rescue the crew, unfortunately the ship was soon broken-up by the pounding of the waves, its wreckage scattered across the beach.

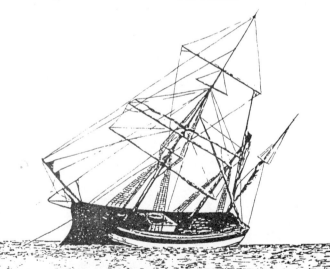

Petrorilia (Belgian barque) grounded on the Chesil Beach 9.12.1856.

THE GREAT STORM OF 1824
THE CARVALHO, UNITY AND EBENEZER
THE STORM NOVEMBER 23rd 1824 LYME REGIS

On the 23rd of November 1824, the south west coast was buffeted by hurricane strong winds. The 'Bristol Gazette' described the storm as "tempest heavy with more frightful terrors is scarcely within the memory of man." The catastrophe to shipping was great. On the Chesil Beach the Danish West Indiaman 'Carvalho' was wrecked, all hands perished, and her cargo of rum, gin and cotton was strewn along the shore. The crew of HMS Ebenezer were more fortunate, so powerful were the waves that she was thrown high up, onto the Chesil Beach. Her only casualty was the master, dashed overboard. The ship was so far from the sea that it was easier to drag her to the Weymouth side of Beach for relaunching. At Abbotsbury a Danish brig was washed ashore and her crew of five saved. At Fleet the waves crashed over the Chesil Beach, raising the level of the lagoon by over twenty feet, flooding houses and drowning many who lived at the back of the Chesil.

Lyme Regis suffered badly, the harbour walls were breached a revenue cutter was swept out of the harbour and sank, the crew drowned. Other boats and ships washed out of the protection of the harbour were able to ride out the storm. A London trader the Unity was well tied to the Cobb wall, but the bollard broke under the strain. The crew set the aft sail to provide some steerage, but the trader drifted towards the cliffs to the east of the town, driven on by the strong winds. The event was watched by the townsfolk, unable to do anything. The crew climbed into the rigging as the ship beached. A local man, Captain Bennet seeing the plight grabbed some rope and raced to the top of the cliffs. A rope was fixed and thrown to the 'Unity' and the crew were rescued.

The sea is recorded at the time as being two hours ahead of itself as the wind drove up through the Channel. Numerous ships were recorded lost, much property was damaged and many drowned.

FISHING SMACK WRECKED ON LAUNCH!
ELIZA   LYME REGIS
(Fishing Smack)   1824

The Eliza must have been one of the fastest shipwrecks ever. She had only just been built and awaited launching, from a boatyard at Lyme Regis. When a severe south westerly gale blew up. The storm swept seas crashing up into the boatyard, which was then situated to the west of the Cobb. The Eliza was nearly finished and was on its launching stocks. The sudden crash of water, swept the stocks away and launched the newly built smack, though no sconer was in floating than it crashed into the rocks and broke up.

FISHING SMACK SWEPT TO DESTRUCTION
CAROLINE   1824   LYME REGIS
(Fishing Smack, 16 tons)

It was a stormy day and the waves were crashing over the high wall of the Cobb, Lyme Regis. The fishing smack Caroline broke her moorings from the harbour and was soon swept out. She eventually grounded at the mouth of the Buddle, becoming wedged underneath the bridge, and with the large waves crashing into her, she soon broke up.

REVENUE MEN DROWNED
FOX   1824   LYME REGIS
(Revenue Cutter)

The revenue cutter Fox was washed out of the confines of the harbour during the great storm on the

22nd of November, 1824. The cutter was moored to the side of the Cobb. The wind was blowing a gale from the southwest. By 1 a.m. the tide had started to flow, though low tide was not till an hour later. By 5 a.m. the tide had passed the high water mark two hours ahead of its estimated time. The wind blew at speeds of hurricane force. At dawn after a pounding through the night a breach appeared in the high wall, allowing the full force of the waves to crash into the harbour. The Revenue cutter Fox strained and broke her moorings, the cutter being swept into the swirling rough sea. She soon broke up on the rocks and ledges to the east of the town her two crew being drowned. The London based trader 'The Unity' also washed out from the harbour, was more fortunate (see Unity).

"CUSTOMS AND REVENUE MEN DROWN"
THE HEROINE   1852   LYME REGIS
    The Heroine was a barque that got into difficulties off Lyme Regis, during a fierce southwesterly gale. She attempted to make for the shelter of the harbour, but hit the rocks on the approach. A rescue boat manned by customs men from the revenue cruiser Frances, attempted to guide the ship into the harbour, but was overcome by the large waves. Four of the would be rescuers were drowned and only one survived, named William Bridle. Mr. Bridle was later awarded a silver medal for his efforts, and a fund was set up for the families of the drowned men. The passengers on the Heroine managed to reach shore in the ships own boats. Because of the disaster it was decided to station a permanent lifeboat at Lyme Regis.

LIFE BOAT MAN KILLED
JEUNE ROSE   1854   LYME REGIS
(French brigatine)
    On January 7th 1854 a fierce southwest gale was

blowing. During the storm the cargo of the French ship shifted allowing the waves to pour water into the holds. The ship was spotted in distress from the town and the lifeboat was launched, manned by the coastguard. They reached the vessel rowing through the storm, and climbed on board to see if it was possible to sail the vessel to safety. A large wave hit the boat, and combined with the shift of cargo it made her roll over, capsizing the lifeboat that lay alongside. The five men in the boat were able to scramble clear, though one of the coastguard was drowned. The lifeboat righted itself, and the rest of the crew from the French vessel were rescued.

COURAGEOUS RESCUE BY LYME LIFEBOAT

ELIZABETH ANN   1860   LYME REGIS (coal smack).

On the 14th of November the Lyme Regis Lifeboat made a daring rescue of the crew of the Elizabeth Ann. She was a coal carrying smack that got into difficulties to the back of the Cobb, during strong westerly winds. She was driven onto the rocks. The lifeboat was launched, though in order to rescue the crew she had to row between the rocks. The lifeboat crew fended off the side of the lifeboat with oars. The crew of three from the smack were saved.

SEATON IRONMONGER SAVES CARGO

BERA   7th OCTOBER 1896 LYME REGIS (barque)

The Bera was a Finnish trader, which was carrying a cargo of timber. She ran aground on the rocks at Charton Bay, which is between Lyme Regis and Seaton. The ship soon broke up and her load of timber was scattered all along the shore. An enterprising ironmonger from Seaton, together with three of his friends walked from the town to the wreck with a hammer and large bag of nails. By the afternoon they had constructed a large raft from the debris timber, which they then dragged back to Seaton. The next day they set off back to Charton bay with 150 fathoms of rope and three seine nets. The timber was netted and the salvaged cargo was slowly kedged back to Seaton. There is little to be seen of the wreck though some traces can be seen at low tide, of the wooden ribs.

BAY GITANO TORPEDOED TWO MILES OFF LYME REGIS
S.S. BAYGITANO 3,073 TONS   LYME REGIS
1918

The Baygitano fell victim to one of the German submarines lurking off the Dorset coast during the First World War. The Baygitano was a British registered ship, carrying coal. She was torpedoed 1½ miles south west of the Cobb, at Lyme Regis. The torpedoes struck her in the engine room killing three, though five of the crew were successfully rescued. The ship soon sunk, becoming a favourite wreck for divers and anglers, though much salvage has been done on the wreck there are still plenty of parts to see, particularly the boilers and twisted plates.

An eye witness account of the sinking was described to Mr Fowles, the curator of Lyme Regis museum, by Mr. Homyer.

"I got home the night before the sinking, on leave. I was having a lie in when I heard a loud explosion. Looking out of the window I saw one of the fishermen running past, pulling on his sea-jersey." "What is it Frank?" I said "A ship has been torpedoed off the Cobb." So I went down to the harbour, it was coming in thick fog. The lifeboat went out with a scratch crew. The lifeboat crew took their jumpers off, so that they

17

wouldn't look like a naval boat. It was a lovely flat calm sea. The rowing boats went out and brought the crew in. The submarine surfaced and talked to the rowing boats, and asked where the captain of the torpedoed vessel was. He happened to be in the boat they spoke to. So they said, he was in one of the boats that had gone ashore. The submarine Captain wanted to know the name of the ship, that he had sunk.

At the time there were no guns at Lyme capable of inflicting any damage to the submarine. Another witness described the large number of people on the Cobb watching the incident, and that after the sinking only the masts protruded above the water."

TRAWLER WRECKED BETWEEN LYME REGIS AND SEATON

THE FAIRWAY   1978   LYME REGIS

The Fairway was bound from the Channel Islands to Devon. During the voyage her engines broke down. Unable to repair or steer the trawler the Torbay Lifeboat took off the crew. The stricken vessel drifted across Lyme Bay eventually being washed ashore near Culverhole Point. An isolated stretch of coast between Seaton and Lyme Regis. Attempts were made to refloat the trawler, with no success, though many fittings and equipment were salvaged. The trawler was later sold as scrap metal to a Seaton man for £150. In an attempt to break the vessel up explosives were used, also a tractor helping in the salvage work became stuck on the beach and eventually swamped by the incoming tide. There is still plenty of debri left on the beach, for those wishing to visit the site.

"RELIANCE" (ketch) 4th June, 1949. Became trapped in a cave on Portland Bill.

VESSEL HOLED AND SINKS

TROIS ASIS   1817   WEST BAY
(Schooner)

The 19th of January was a fierce day. The wind was blowing from the south west. The Trois Amis tried to make for Bridport Harbour, as it was then known. Though soon grounded it was holed and sunk. Only one of her crew survived.

S.S. PAULINE SANK AT WEST BAY

S.S. PAULINE   1861   WEST BAY
(brigantine, 130 tons).

The Pauline sank on the 9th of September 1861, after going aground at West Bay during a south-west gale. The following account comes from a local newspaper of the time. Which describes the full drama.

Wreck at the harbour. — During the whole of Wednesday morning and afternoon a strange vessel evidently in difficulties was observed tacking about the bay, from which it would have been exceedingly difficult if not impossible to escape, owing to a strong

19

south-west wind which was blowing. At length the she arrived between 4 and 5' O'clock in the afternoon. Just as she was about to enter a heavy sea struck her and drove her to the eastwards, so that instead of passing between the piers, she ran stern on against the east pier. The large solid pile that forms the very extremity of the pier, was much splintered by the shock, while the bowstrip of the vessel was broken off short. After striking, the stern swung round to eastwards, and the ship was soon on the sands, with her broadside to the sea, in a few yards of the pier. The wind was blowing hard from the south-west, and there was a fearful surf running between the ship and the land. The sea beat over her decks and her crew of four men and a boy, sought refuge in the rigging on the land side. Ropes were at once thrown to them and with some difficulty, the whole of the poor fellows were not to land, two of them being pulled up the side of the pier, and the other three dragged through the surf. The ship proved to be the brigantine 'Pauline', of Bayonne in the south of France, of about 130tons burden, laden with corn and bound for Hull. Not one of the crew could speak English. Owing to the shock caused by the vessel's striking the against the pier-head, her masts and rigging were much injured. Both the ten masts broke-off, destroying much of the tackling in their fall. The build of the vessel was much admired by the men of the harbour. She was said to be about three years old, and very strongly built. Captain T. Jarvis, of Bridport Harbour and Captain F. James, of The Good Intent, deserve great praise for the exertions they made, at risk to their own lives, to rescue the poor fellows that clung to the wreck. Part of the cargo has been got out, but the vessel is still lying on the beach. The is in a very bad state, the cargo being all damaged by the water."

BLACK DIAMOND RUNS AGROUND AT WEST BAY

BLACK DIAMOND	1865	WEST BAY
(Scooner)		(Bridport)

Another vessel to meet a similar fate to that of the Alioth was the schooner called 'Black Diamond'. She ran aground entering the harbour with a cargo of oats from Ireland for the Bull Hotel. Five years later the 'Kennet' grounded in the same position. The co-incidence was strange as she was also carrying a cargo of oats for the Bull Hotel, Bridport. Both vessels became total wrecks.

WESTBAY PIER SINKS SHIP

OLIVE	1868	WEST BAY
(Match)		(Bridport)

The Olive was one of the many small vessels that used to trade up and down the coast, carrying general cargo. On January 12th the Olive was homeward bound for London, carrying a cargo of grit and stone, picked up at West Bay. What little wind there was died as soon as she cast off, and the Olive drifted into the piers, where she was quickly holed and sank. A fisherman was drowned the next day, while attempting to board the wreck.

MARIE LEOCADT FOUNDERS AFTER HITTING WEST BAY BAR

MARIE LEOCADT	1868	WEST BAY
(Sailing Vessel)		

The Marie Leocadt was anchored off West Bay waiting for the flooding tide before she could enter and deliver her cargo of coal. The wind was increasing and blowing from the south west, which made it impossible to enter the harbour, as the large waves surged down the channel between the two piers. The captain unable to sail for a safer anchorage decided to stay put. With the worsening weather his anchor dragged. At last he decided to make a desperate run for the harbour, unfortunately a bank of gravel had built up across the harbour leaving very little depth. (A problem that has plagued West Bay to this day). The ship struck the bar, and broke up. Luckily none of the crew were drowned, though the wreck sealed off the harbour channel for two weeks.

DEMETRIUS   1869   WEST BAY
    In January 1869 during a fierce storm the Demetrius grounded and broke up on the East Beach at West Bay. The wreck attracted many onlookers some of whom came far too close to the boiling sea. One of whom, Mr. Gundry being swept away by a large wave.

BRITAINS FIRST EURO M.P.!
'A BALLOON'
THE SALADIN   1881   LYME BAY
    One of the strangest wrecks somewhere in Lyme Bay, is that of a balloon, though I doubt if anything of it now remains. The story starts in Bath, on a cold day in December. The army had recently aquired balloons, for the purpose of observation, and Captain Templar of the Royal Engineers with another officer and Hon. Walter Powell, the member of Parliament for the West Country proposed to go for a demonstration flight.
    While airborne a fresh breeze caught the balloonists unaware, and soon they were blown away from Bath across Somerset and into Dorset. The coast soon loomed into view, and Captain Templar decided the only course of action was to release some of the air, and crash land. They came down in a field near West Bay. The impact threw the two officers out

of the basket. Unfortunately, the Honorable Walter Powell M.P. was not quick enough, to scramble clear, and the balloon was once again airborne, carrying the unfortunate Member of Parliament. The balloon vanished out to sea, and though the Lyme Regis Lifeboat spent many hours searching, no trace of the balloon or passenger could be found.

Perhaps the Honourable Walter Powell M.P. went on to become Britains first unrequested Euro M.P.!

The schooner "ARDENTE" aground in Weymouth Bay — December 1914

LACK OF 50p WRECKS SHIP

ALIOTH   1923   WEST BAY
(Iron clad sailing vessel)   (Bridport)

The Alioth was one of the many small sailing

23

vessels that delivered and took cargos to and from Bridport. The German ship had delivered timber and was taking a cargo of local sand. The Captain, an impatient man wished to sail, though the wind was blowing from the south. A local boat offered a tow out of the harbour for the price of 50p. (as was common practice). The captain refused and then set about pushing his ship out of the port by the use of oars and poles. No sooner had he cleared the harbour than he ran aground, the incoming tide failed to float the vessel which was now stranded on the east beach. The wind increased, the waves smashing into the ship and in a short time the ship was wrecked. An expensive mistake for not taking a tow!

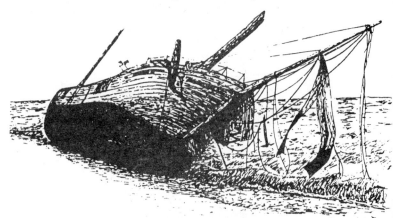

Russian Schooner "EMMA MARIE" breaking up on the Chesil Beach, 1903.

THE GOLD BULLION WRECK

HOPE (OR HOOP)   1765   CHESIL BEACH
(Dutch East Indiaman)

The most valuable and richest cargos to be washed up on the shores of the Chesil was that of the Hoop. She was a Dutch East Indiaman of 350 tons.

The Hoop was caught off the Chesil in a southwest gale, and driven onto the shore. The mast cracked and fell onto the beach allowing the crew to scramble onto the shore. The wreck attracted a sizable group who soon discovered among its varied cargo, gold bullion and jewels. The wreck was taken over by the plunderers, attracting large crowds from the surrounding towns and villages. The alcohol among the cargo was soon consumed, with some of the villagers passing out on the shore; later to die from exposure. Squabbles developed among rival gangs for the loot, and one man was stabbed in a fight. The rioting and looting was eventually stopped by the militia from Dorchester, and a subsequent search of houses around Portland recovered much of the looted gold and jewellery. Not all of the cargo valued at £70,000 was recovered and much probably still lies under the Chesil Beach, waiting to be found!

MILITARY CONVOY WRECKED ON CHESIL

THE LOSS OF THE THOMAS, VENUS, PIEDMONT, GOLDEN GROVE, AEOLUS AND HANNA CATHERINE.
1795   Chesil Beach

One of the Worst disasters on the Chesil Beach took place in late November 1795. A squadron of ships, under the command of Rear Admiral Hugh Christian, set sail for the West Indies, carrying a varied cargo of troops, horses military ordinance and general supplies. A merchantman 'The Golden Grove' joined the convoy as it sailed down the Channel from Portsmouth. The squadron was well west of Portland near Torbay when the south-west winds began to increase; rather than venture on, the Admiral hoisted flags for the ships to make for the shelter of Spithead.

In the appallingly bad weather the convoy broke up, part of the flotilla found its self blown off the Chesil beach, near West Bay. Anchors were dropped in a desperate bid to stop the ships grounding, but to no avail. The Aeolus was spotted by the militia as she drifted onto the the shore. Nine of her crew made a desperate attempt to reach the land but drowned. A large wave soon hit the ship, pushing and leaving her high up on the bank of shingle. The other nine of her crew survived. Shortly after the Aeolus the Golden Grove was driven ashore. The Golden Grove was a general cargo vessel, not part of the convoy, but using its protection for a safer passage the Oporto. Of the crew, five drowned and eighteen survived.

Further to the west along the Chesil the other vessels in the convoy were in serious trouble. The Thomas, another merchantman lost thirteen of its crew and sixteen were saved. On the Hannah all the crew were saved. The two worst casualties were the Venus of whom only 18 survived out of its crew 110 and the Piedmont, a military troop ship on whom 139 drowned.

The total deaths caused by the storm were 298, also a number of horses which came from the wreck of the Catherine. An eye witness at the time describes the scene....." To give a true description of the horror I have witnessed would be impossible...consider a transport with near two hundred troops on board sinking within fifty yards of the shore, the cries distinctly heard and the bodies floating on the waves, but the means of affording assistance unpracticable. Of the two hundred, ten lives are saved by the waves throwing the bodies on to the beach......"

The calamity left the Chesil strewn with wreckage and bodies from the stricken ship. Many of the bodies were buried in a communal grave at Wyke Regis.

WRECKERS PILFER SHIP AT WYKE REGIS

THE ALEXANDER   1815   CHESIL BEACH
(East Indiaman)

On Easter Monday the 27th of March 1815, the East Indiaman returning home from Bombay was driven ashore in a south-westerly gale. The ship came ashore at Wyke Regis only five people survived the catastrophe. 155 passengers and crew drowned. The ships cargo of cotton, sugar, coffee, tea, pepper and rice disappeared at the hands of the local wreckers, and little was recovered except some of the mail. One body from the wreck was washed up at Lyme Regis. It was thought to be that of Lady Jackson, returning home from India with her children. It was a sad and tragic ending to the four month voyage, when they were so near home.

Sixty of the dead are buried at a communal grave near South Gate, St. Georges, Portland.

STORM CLAIMS IMMIGRANT SHIP

THE ROYAL ADELAIDE   1872   CHESIL BEACH
(1,385 Tons Iron Built Clipper)

The Royal Adelaide was an immigrant ship bound for Sidney Australia. The weather was bad as she rounded Portland Bill on the night of the 24th November; the wind strong with bad visability, with southwest winds not blowing, the captain decided to seek the shelter of Portland. Due to the conditions, the Captain incorrectly interpreted his position and was soon off the Chesil Beach, near the ferry bridge, instead of near Lulworth Cove to the east of Portland Bill as he assumed. The coastguard lit flares from the beach to warn the Captain of the danger. The anchors were lowered to try and ride out the storm, but to no avail as they dragged in the severe conditions. Soon the ship ran aground, the pounding breaking the ship's back. The vessel rolled broadside onto the shore. The first mate bravely took a line in an attempt to swim to the shore but was drowned. The coastguard were able to put a line onto the ship with their rocket equipment, but the passengers, afraid of the sea would not trust the line. The Captain went first with a small child and reached the shore and, the apparatus rescued sixty before the line snapped. Slowly the ship broke up and those left on board were swept away by the sea. In total only seven were drowned, the casualties would have been much worse if it had not been for the mortar apparatus of the Portland Coastguard.

A major benefit of the wreck was the cargo of soap, coffee, sugar, cloth, brandy, gin and rum which was soon washed onto the beach and eagerly gathered up.

RUSSIAN CREW HAVE LUCKY ESCAPE
EMMA MARIE   1903   CHESIL BEACH
(Schooner)

The Emma Marie was wrecked on the Chesil Beach on Sunday the 25th of October. The Russian schooner had left Teignmouth, loaded with a cargo of china clay, bound for Lisbon in Portugal. Unfortunately shortly after leaving the port the wind blew force from a south westerly direction. With the rough seas and high wind the 'Emma' was blown off course, across Lyme Bay. From West Bay the schooner was seen to be flying distress signals. Three tugs set out from Portland, one of which, the Petra was able to get a line on board and started to tow the stricken vessel to safety, but due to the rough seas the tow line snapped and the 'Petra' sustained damage and was unable to complete the tow. She left the Russian ship anchored off Blacknor Point, but the heavy pounding she received soon snapped her anchors. The Emma Marie, once more adrift was thrown onto the Chesil Beach; her sails and rigging in tatters. At the height of the storm the mast snapped, falling from the ship onto the beach, forming a bridge to safety. With little time to save themselves the crew scrambled from the ship, down the mangled mast and onto the chesil, with no loss of life or injury. A very lucky escape from disaster. The ship was winter off, and broke up in the surf.

'GREEK STEAMSHIP GROUNDED ON THE CHESIL'

S.S. PREVEZA   1920   CHESIL

In the winter of 1920 the Greek Steamship Preveza, ran aground on the Chesil Beach during thick fog. At first it was thought they could save the steamer and a tug was sent round from Portland. The tug tried several attempts to tow off the grounded vessel. On the fourth attempt the tug became entangled in its own anchor cable, which wrapped

"PREVEZA", wrecked 15th January, 1920.
Chesil Cove, Portland.

29

IDENTIFIED WRECKS IN LYME BAY

DEVON

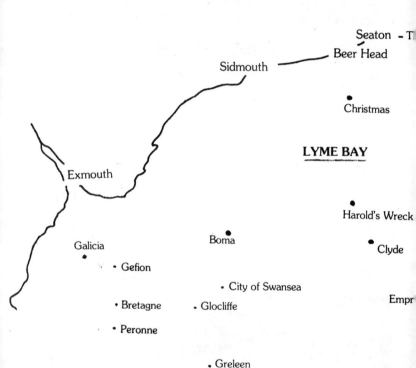

Seaton - T

Beer Head

Sidmouth

Christmas

LYME BAY

Exmouth

Harold's Wreck

Clyde

Galicia

Boma

Empr

• Gefion

• City of Swansea

• Bretagne   . Glocliffe

• Peronne

. Greleen

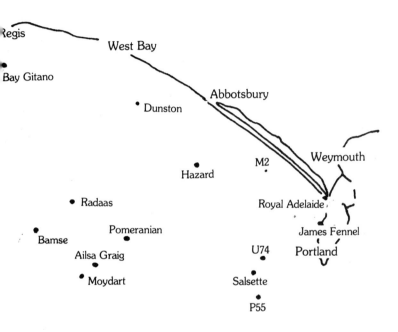

DORSET

Regis

● Bay Gitano

West Bay

Abbotsbury

● Dunston

Weymouth

● Hazard

M2

Royal Adelaide

● Radaas

James Fennel

Pomeranian

● Bamse

Portland

U74

Ailsa Graig

● Moydart

Salsette

P55

hese wrecks can be dived".

around the propeller. The tug only just managed to save itself from the same fate as the Preveza. The ship was left to await higher tides before trying to refloat her. A subsequent storm severely damaged the ship, before a second attempt could be made. It was eventually decided to break the ship up on the beach. For many years afterwards the ship's boilers could be seen on the Chesil bank.

WRECKED VESSEL SOLD FOR £1

MADELAINE TRISTAN   1930   CHESIL BEACH
(Three Masted Schooner)

The Madelaine Tristan was a handsome three masted schooner. She was in ballast and travelling to Le Harve. The schooner at one time had been the mother ship to the French fishing fleet that fished the waters of Newfoundland; so she was sturdy and well built. She was driven ashore by the fierce south-west winds that were blowing on the 20th of September. Her crew scrambled ashore. The Madelaine Tristan was thrown on the beach at Chesil cove.

The schooner was eventually sold for £1 as scrap, though only her masts were removed. Her hull became a local landmark, till it was broken up by the council as she had become infested with rats and was a health hazard.

LANDING CRAFT COUGHT IN STORM

TANK LANDING CRAFT   1944   CHESIL BEACH
(LC (T) 2454)

It was on October 13th and early Autumn that the tank landing craft manned by the Royal Navy got into difficulties off the Chesil Beach during a southwest gale. The navy dispatched a tug from Portland, but the sea was too rough for it to come round the Bill. The lifeboat rounded the Bill and was soon at the scene. No sooner had she arrived and was preparing to take off the crew than she was ordered to stand off by the coastguard, on the shore. They judged that the conditions were so rough, that the lifeboat would be smashed by the waves while alongside the landing craft. The coastguard used their rocket apparatus, and were able to fire a line onto the craft. They successfully rescued three ratings, before a large wave washed away the line apparatus drowning two of the attending coastguards, and leaving the nine remaining crew to their fate on the landing craft. In total eleven lives were lost.

WORDSWORTH'S BROTHER DROWNED
EARL OF ABERGAVENNY 1805   PORTLAND

One of the most tragic sinkings off the Dorset coast was the Loss of the Earl of Abergavenny. The Abergavenny was an East Indiaman of 1,200 imperial tons. Her captain was John Wordsworth, the brother of the poet William Wordsworth.

The ship left Portsmouth on February 1st 1805 bound for India and onto China. A trading mission which, if successful, would have made John Wordsworth and his backers a healthy profit. The ship carried a large cargo and over 400 passengers and crew, including 160 new recruits for the East India Company army, thirty chinese and sixty ordinary passengers.

The Earl of Abergavenny set out in convoy with four other vessels. During the voyage the weather deteriorated and the ships sought shelter behind Portland. While sheltering, the Abergavenny drifted onto the Shambles. The wind had died, and there was no danger. Captain Wordsworth waited for the tide to

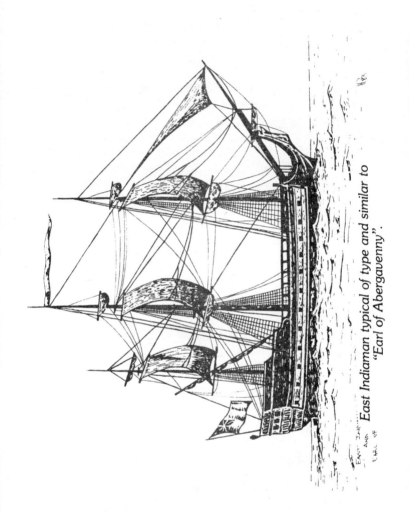

East Indiaman typical of type and similar to "Earl of Abergavenny".

34

float him free. The wind increased and the Abergavenny pounded the bottom. The ships carpenter found a leak in one of the holds, which soon filled with water, despite desperate pumping. The ship settled back onto the sand of the shambles. There was still no immediate danger as the sea was still moderate. The purser was sent with the ships papers; two lady passengers and six crew to go and seek aid for the stricken ship. The sailors were encouraged to man the pumps by a free issue of grog, It was not till 9.00 p.m. that the passengers were told of the predicament. By then, the weather had worsened considerably and there was little hope of using the ships lifeboats. At 11 p.m. the ship sank, many were drowned in the icy winter waters, others climbed into the rigging which rose out of the sea. It was not until an hour later that any rescue was attempted. A local sloop came close and rescued many who clung to the spars and ropes. By daybreak, the full extent of the tradgedy was revealed. Two hundred and thirty three people had drowned; Captain Wordsworth also went down with his ship, his body being recovered a month later on the beach at Weymouth. The local beaches were straggled with the clothes and remains of the ship. The bodies of many that were drowned were buried in a mass grave at Wyke Regis. Salvage attempts were made to rescue the cargo, which were only partially successful. Much still remains to be discovered.

*The Paddle Steamer "BOURNEMOUTH",
broken on rocks at Portland in 1886*

METEOR HITS PORTLAND STONE

S.S.METEOR   1830   **PORTLAND**
(Packet Paddle Steamer)   (Church Ope Cove)

Fog is as much the enemy of the mariner, as strong winds. On the 23rd of February, the Meteor, a Royal Mail Packet paddle steamer, bound for the Channel Islands from Weymouth, ran aground, on the rocks at Ope Cove, during thick fog. The first mate, Edward Thresher, struggled ashore with a line, and soon all the the passengers were safely on land and not a crew member lost. Later that night over one hundred Portlanders climbed onto the vessel and took all the luggage, proving that old customs die hard, and that wrecking and salvage were Gods gift to the windswept people of Portland, and what was placed on the shore would not remain there long either from the elements or man. And in the Portlanders case, usually man!

"MYRTLEDENE", wrecked on 25th March, 1912.
On the rocks at Portland.

37

AVALANCHE HIT BY FALLING FOREST

S.S. AVALANCE   1877   PORTLAND
IRON CLAD SAILING SHIP COLLISION WITH THE S.S. FOREST

Sailors are superstitious and more so in the days of sail, when it was the power of the wind that dictated your departure, journey and arrival. It was not a good omen to the crew of the Avalanche when she lost her figurehead in an early collision with a barge while coming down the Thames.

The Avalanche was bound for New Zealand, with a crew of thirty-four, and sixty-four passengers. The Avalanche was iron built, and carried a general cargo of goods worth in total £100,000.

On Tuesday the 11th September, a few miles off Portland, the weather was raining with mist. The watch spotted lights from the bridge, it was the S.S. Forest, a Canadian registered sailing vessel, in ballast ballast with a crew of 21. The two ships were on opposite tacks. The Forest on a starboard tack had right of way, and burnt flares to warn the Avalanche of his approach. It was to no avail, neither Captain took evasive courses. The Forest struck the Avalanche amidship, rebounding from the first impact under full sail she drove once more into the stern of the Avalanche. The Avalanche with large gashes in her side, sank quickly. All on board the Avalanche, were drowned, except for the 3rd mates and two Seamen, who scrambled from the Avalanche onto the Forest, during the collision.

The Forest was also damaged and started to ship water through a large hole in the bow. Captain Lockhart ordered the crew to abandon ship. The three lifeboats were launched, though some of the crew in the confusion, were left on board. Of the three boats, only one reached the safety of Portland. The collision was a disaster and 102 people were drowned. A memorial Church was built to the victims at Southwell Cliff Portland, from donations sent in by the public.

The hulk of the Forest continued to float in the Channel, and was eventually blown up by the Royal Navy.

"MINERVE", wrecked 19th September, 1945.
Near Portland Bill.

THE COLLISION OF THE WAITARA AND HURANUI

WAITARA AND THE S.S. HURANUI
22nd JUNE 1883   PORTLAND

The Waitara and the Huranui were both iron clad sailing vessels and owned by the New Zealand Shipping Company. They were sailing from London to Wellington in New Zealand. The weather off Portland

39

in early summer was bad with low visibility. The two ships sailing in convoy, were at the time on opposite tacks, as they fought into the south-west wind, blowing up the Channel. It soon became apparent that the ships were on a collision course, though due to the bad visibility it was too late to avoid the inevitable. The Hurunui struck the Waitara in the middle, stoving in planks, and creating such a large hole, that the ship sunk with-in three minutes. Few of the passangers or crew had a chance to escape and twenty-seven people drowned.

NAVY SINKS OWN SUBMARINE

L24 SUBMARINE   1924   PORTLAND
It was early January when the British Atlantic fleet sailed from Portland Harbour. Five miles west of Portland Bill the British submarine L24 was rammed by HMS Resolution and quickly sank, drowning forty three crewmen. A worse disaster nearly happened when two other submarines collided and the HMS Ramillies, a battleship struck Portland breakwater.

Submarine M2, lost off Chesil 1932.

THE M2 FAILS TO SURFACE

M2 SUBMARINE   1932
The M2 was a large submarine and some what of a disaster in design, incorporating an aircraft hanger in the bow section of the vessel with two large hanger doors. The submarine carried a small seaplane. A

considerable performance and effort, coinciding with the right conditions was needed to launch the plane. The M2 put out from Portland on a training mission. It dived at a spot west of Portland, and failed to surface. The site is in a 100ft of water and frequently dived, the hanger doors after the accident were found to be slightly open flooding the submarine and drowning the crew.

HOLED TRAWLER SLIDES OFF ROCKS

S.S. JAMES FENNEL 1945   PORTLAND
(Admiralty Steam Trawler)

The James Fennel had sailed from Gibralter bound for Portsmouth. On the 21st of January while sailing in thick fog, she struck rocks off Blacknor Point, at Portland. The crew were able to escape but the trawler was holed, then slid off the rocks and settled in 60ft of water. The trawler is still in one piece and is frequently visited by local divers.

MISSING MAURITAN RUPEES AND WRECKED RANGE ROVERS

AEOLIAN SKY   1979   PORTLAND

The Aeolian Sky is one of the most recent wrecks off the Dorset coast. She was a general cargo carrier bound from London to Nigeria, carrying Trains, Range Rovers, Cloth and Mauritian Ruppees and miscellaneous goods. While sailing down the English Channel she collided with the Anna Knueppal, a German registered ship of 1,000 tons. The Aeolian Sky was holed and leaking. The Captain tried to make for the nearest harbour but sank 12 miles east of Portland the next day. The Anna Knueppel was not badly damaged and was able to make port.

The Government issued a warning that the vessel, The Aeolian Sky, was carrying dangerous unspecified chemicals. This would seem to have been a ploy to keep divers off the wreck, till the salvage could start to recover the goods and the large sum of Mauritian money. When salvage divers entered the ship they found the money had already gone from the safe.

The ship has since been extensively salvaged. Her propellers were brought up in 1980. The navy demolished some of the top structure as it was a hazard to shipping. The ship is lying in 95ft of water off St. Albans Head. Divers should be aware of strong tides, though there is still much to see.

THE STORY OF THE 'WELFARE', STATE

THE WELFARE   1371   KIMMERIDGE

The story of the Welfare shows that it was not only the Portlanders that helped themselves to wrecks and looted ships. The Welfare ran ashore in fine weather on the beach at Kimmeridge; though in no imminent danger they waited to refloat the ship. The wreckers rights at the time were owned by the Abbey of Cerne, who would prefer to have a wreck, than a whole ship. In order to obtain a wreck the monks 'persuaded' the crew to abandon the ship, which in the interests of their own health, they did. The Abbey then claimed the resulting 'wreck', preceeded to take or loot its cargo of silks and gold cloth. An owner, some what peeved at loosing his chattels to gods men on earth complained. The resulting inquiry found the Abbey guilty of permitting stolen goods to be housed on its land, though it does not say if the man reclaimed his goods.

166 DIE ON SEACOMBE CLIFFS

HALSWELL   6th JANUARY 1786 KIMMERIDGE
(Seacombe Cliffs)

The S.S. Halswell was an East Indiaman, en route

from England to Calcutta (India), in the early winter of 1786. Her journey down the channel, from her home port of Gravesend was slow, the weather atrocious. The wind was from the south west, and the sea crashed over the deck of the ship.

Near St. Alban's head the ship's planking sprang a leak, filling the cargo hold with water. Steerage became impossible, and it was decided to chop down the main mast, to prevent the ship turning over in the swell. A jury rig, was arranged so that the Halsewell could sail back towards Studland Point, and protection from the southwest winds. The Halsewell seemed to be winning, as she avoided the race off St. Alban's Head, but the wind still pushed her further towards the shore. The sea and visability were bad and soon the cliffs at Seacombe (a few miles to the east of Kimmeridge) loomed into view. In desperation, the captian lowered the anchors, to try and ride the storm out, but the anchors would not hold. The ship struck the base of the cliffs with aloud explosion, the timbers grinding and breaking on the rocks. Those that were not drowned, managed to climb onto the base of the cliffs, where there was a small cave that provided some shelter from the bitter winds. As yet, no alarm had been given on land. It was not till much later that two seamen were able to scale the cliffs and seek help. Local quarrymen, rescued the last of the survivors some twenty-four hours after the start of the disaster. Of the 242 passengers and crew on board the Halsewell, only 76 survived and 166 were drowned, or died from exposure. The beach was strewn with the wreckage from the vessel, which had been well provisioned for its journey to the East. The quarrymen of Seacombe were rewarded by the company for their help, for without them many more would have died.

S.S. TREVEAL, FIASCO

S.S. TREVEAL   KIMMERIDGE
9th JAN 1920

The S.S. Treveal was on route from Calcutta to Dundee with a cargo of jute and ore. She came up the Channel with out a pilot, and in bad visibility made an error in her position, so laying a course which eventually led her onto the ledges of Kimmeridge. The Treveal struck the ledges on 9th of January 1920. There was no panick. Little damage had been done, and the Captain sent a signal for a tug to come and tow them off. By morning no tug had arrived and the weather started to deteriorate. The waves were pounding into the side of the ship and there was a great danger of the vessel breaking up. The Captain gave the order to abandon ship, though did not realize that the Weymouth lifeboat was en route and not far away. In swell and storm the ships lifeboat capsized and 36 passengers and crew were drowned. The coastguard were found to have been negligent in their duty and one member was disciplined and dismissed from the service.

NEW SHIP CREATED FROM OLD

S.S. BRITISH INVENTOR   ST. ALBANS HEAD
(steam tanker)   1940

The British Inventor was a victim of a sea mine, on the 13th of June, 1940. She struck the mine in calm waters. Disabled she floated towards the shambles. The lifeboat was launched from Portland, though an armed naval yacht reached her first and managed to take off the 25 crew members. The British Inventor was still afloat and Admiralty tugs tried in vain to tow her into Portland, but by late afternoon the tanker had taken in too much water and she foundered and sank,

5 miles off St. Albans Head. The aft section of the British Inventor was later salvaged and a new forward section built. Today the debris of the ships remains scattered on the sea floor.

"CHRISTIANE" (Norwegian barque) 1883.
Grounded on the Chesil Beach.

ARMY BALLOON SINKS IN LYME BAY

BALLOON   13th MAY 1907   EXMOUTH

The Skylark was a fishing vessel out from Brixham, working the grounds 7 miles to the south east of Exmouth. While fishing, the skipper spotted a large ball object floating on the surface of the water. With interest aroused, the fishing boat chased after the ball, which was still being blown about, by the wind. After a chase lasting five hours, they managed to catch the ball, which they discovered to be a balloon. The wicker basket was still attached to the rigging, and inside contained an officers riding crop. With nothing of value, the fishermen stowed the balloon in a hold and resumed fishing, and did not land their catch at Brixam till three days later. The salvaged balloon was handed over to the authorities, who after inquiries discovered that the balloon had set off from Aldershot (in Hampshire); on board were two officers of the Royal Engineers, on a trail flight. A sea search was launched but no trace of the two officers was ever found.

———————

NAME	DATE OF SINKING	HOW	POSITION	GENERAL
Aeolus	11.1795	Grounded	Chesil (near Ferry Bridge)	
Ada	1898	Grounded	Kimmeridge	
Aeolion Sky	3.11.1979	Collision	Portland Bill (12 miles east)	
Agnes	19. 3.1838	Grounded	Sidmouth	
Agreement (American Trader)	1680	Grounded	Weymouth Bay	Cargo of animal skins
Ailsa Craig (601 Tons)	15. 4.1918	Torpedoed	Portland Bill (13 miles west by north)	Coal
Albion (Schooner)	12. 3.1903	Holed	West Bay	Cargo of Bridport grit
Alexander (East Indiaman)	27. 2.1815	Grounded	Chesil Beach (Nr. Wyke Regis)	Cotton, Coffee, Rice.
Alex Van Opstal (5,900 Tons)	15. 9.1939	Mined	East of Portland Bill	
Belgium Liner				
Alioth (Iron clad sailing ship)	3. 5.1923	Grounded	West Bay (East Beach)	Sand
Amelia (German brig)	1. 2.1869			
Amulet (brig)	28.10.1852		Seaton	
Amy	24. 3.1928			
Amyntas	1824	Grounded	Weymouth Bay	
Angelina (Fishing smack) 80 Tons	1.11 1815	Rocks	Lyme Regis (Church Cliffs)	
Anna-Marie (Russian schooner)	25.10.1903	Grounded	Chesil Beach (Blacknor Point)	
Annie Edwin (Jersey schooner)	1879	Collision	Portland	
Arethusa	24.11.1838	Foundered	Chesil (off the Fleet)	
Arthur Le Juvenale (French brig)	18. 3.1821	Grounded	Chesil	Cotton, Coffee.
Atlas (American brig)	7.12.1831	Grounded	Chesil	

47

NAME	DATE OF SINKING	HOW	POSITION	GENERAL
Avalanche (Iron clad sailing ship)	9.1877	Collision	Portland Bill	General cargo valued at time as £100,000.
Balloon	13. 5.1907	Blown out to sea	Off Exmouth	
Bamburgh (S.S. Gibel-Heman) 6479 tons	14. 9.1918	Torpedoed	Off Abbotsbury	
Bamse 958 tons	17. 4.1918	Torpedoed	Portland Bill (15 miles west by north)	
Bassurella (French Trawler)	15. 7.1963	Foundered	Chesil (Nr. Langton Herring)	
Bay Gitano 3073 tons	2. 2.1918	Torpedoed	Lyme Regis (1½ miles southwest)	Coal
Bee (sloop)	11.1824	Grounded	West Bay	
Bellona (Privateer)	5. 9.1779	Foundered	Teignmouth	
Bera (Finnish sailing vessel)	7.10.1896	Rocks	Lyme Regis/Seaton Chesil	Wood
Bittion HMS (Bittern)				
Binnendijk (Dutch freighter)	7.10.1939	Mined	The Shambles	
Black Diamond	11.1865	Grounded	West Bay	Oats
Black Hawk (American Steamer)	29.12.1944	Torpedoed	Worbarrow	
Bleamoor (Armed merchantman) 3755 tons	27.11.1917	Torpedoed	Berry Head (4 miles S.S.E.)	
Boadicea HMS (Iron clad) Destroyer			Portland Bill	
Boma (Armed merchantman) 2694 tons	11. 6.1918	Torpedoed	Beer Head (10 miles S.W.) Potatoes, Hay, Straw.	

NAME	DATE OF SINKING	HOW	POSITION	GENERAL
Bournemouth (Paddle steamer)	27. 8.1886	Rocks	Portland Bill	
Bretagne (Steamship) 14399 tons	10. 8.1918	Collision	Teignmouth	Coal
British Inventor (Tanker)	13. 6.1940	Mined	St. Albans Head (5 miles off)	
Broomhill 1392 tons	10. 5.1917	Sunk, submarine gunfire	Portland Bill (9 miles S.W.)	
Brothers	16.11.1812	Rocks	Exmouth	
Buccaneer Aircraft				
Buesten (Tanker) 5187 tons (Busston)	9. 4.1941	Bombed	Berry Head	Benzine
Bulow (German)	18. 6.1914		Blacknor Point	
Caroline (Fishing smack) 16 tons	1824	Grounded	Lyme Regis (river mouth)	
Caroline	12. 2.1860	Grounded	Straight Point, Devon	
Caroline of Leigh (36 ft. Yacht)	1979	Foundered	Lulworth (3 miles off)	
Carvalho (Danish West Indiaman)	23.11.1824	Grounded	Chesil	Rum, Cotton.
Catherine HMS (Military transport)	11.1795	Foundered	Chesil	
City of Swansea 1375 tons	25. 9.1917	Torpedoed	Berry Head (15 miles E.N.E.)	
Christiane (Norwegian barque)	2. 9.1883	Grounded	Chesil	
Christmas (Fishing vessel)	1981		Sidmouth	
Clan Macuey	18. 8.1918	Torpedoed	Pool	Coal
Clyde HMS (trawler)	14.10.1917	Collision	Sidmouth	
Collingwood	15. 3.1871		Lyme Regis	
Columbine (schooner)	11.1838	Grounded		

NAME	DATE OF SINKING	HOW	POSITION	GENERAL
Colville (West Indiaman)	23.11.1824	Foundered	West Bay	Wine, Rum, Cotton.
Colyton Union 91½ tons	24.11.1846		Lyme Regis	
Commodore (brigantine)			Exmouth (Encombe Ledge)	
Countess of Erne (paddles steamer)	16. 9.1935		Portland Harbour	
Crown of Denmark	13. 1.1931	Hit Breakwater	Portland	
Delight HMS (Destroyer) 1375 tons	26. 7.1940	Bombed	Portland	
Demetrius	22. 1.1869	Grounded	West Bay (East Beach)	
Dorothea (Dutch steamer)	14. 2.1914		Chesil (Nr. Abbotsbury)	
Dove	11.1838	Grounded	Weymouth Bay	
Dove	3. 1.1872		Branscombe	
Duchess of Devonshire (steamer)	27. 8.1933	Grounded	Sidmouth	
Duchess of York	1780	Grounded	Portland Bill	
Dudley Rose 1600 tons	9. 4.1941		Off Torbay	
Dustan (dredger)	23. 9.1917	Mined	Chesil	
Dwyer (Canadian) 17770 tons WH Tanker	26. 8.1917	Torpedoed	Berry Head (15 miles N.E.)	
Earl of Abergavenny 1200 tons East Indiaman	3. 2.1805	Foundered	The Shambles Cargo valued £70,000	Wedgewood china,
Ebenezer HMS (sloop)	11.1824	Grounded	Chesil Beach	
Edwin & Sarah (ketch)	5. 1.1882	Rocks	Chesil Cove	
Ehen (barque)	4.1890	Grounded	Portland (Mutton Cove)	Rice, Pickles.
Elena R (Greek Steamship) 4500 tons	11.1939	Sank	Nr. The Shambles	

NAME	DATE OF SINKING	HOW	POSITION	GENERAL
Eliza (fishing smack)	1824	Foundered	Lyme Regis	
Elizabeth Ann	14.11.1860	Rocks	Lyme Regis	Coal
Emma & John (Weymouth trawler)	11. 1.1914	Grounded on Cliffs	Lyme Regis	
Emma Marie (Russian schooner)	25.10.1903	Grounded	Chesil Beach	
Emmanuel (French brig)	22.11.1865	Grounded	Chesil Cove	
Empress of India 5585 tons	1.11.1913	Used for target practice	Off Portland west	
Endeavour (brig)	8.1879	Grounded	Burton Bradstock	
Ethel (merchantman) 2336 tons	16. 9.1918	Torpedoed	Berry Head (8 miles S.E.)	
Eugene Schneider (French barque)	2.12.1927	Collision	Portland	
Evertsen (steamship)	24. 6.1961	Collision	Portland	
Fanny C. (schooner)	31.10.1890	Grounded while on fire	Chesil Cove	
Fram (schooner)	1824	Grounded	West Bay	
Fisgard 2. (Naval Training ship)	17. 9.1914	Foundered		
Flirt	1891	Grounded	Burton Bradstock	
Flying Fish	31.10.1881	Rocks	Lyme Regis (The Cobb)	
Forest	11. 9.1877	Collision	Portland Bill (15 miles S.W.)	
Formidable HMS (Battleship) 15000 tons	1.1915	Torpedoed	Start Point, Devon	
Fortuna (Dutch galliot)	19.12.1824	Grounded	Chesil Beach (Nr. Ferry House)	
Fox (schooner)	21. 2.1812	Grounded	West Bay	Some silver coins found
Fox (Revenue Cruiser)	1824	Grounded	Lyme Regis (Cobb Gate)	
Francis Feeling (Mail Packet)	6. 9.1826	Collision	Portland	

NAME	DATE OF SINKING	HOW	POSITION	GENERAL
Frogner 14769 tons	29. 4.1918	Torpedoed	Exmouth	
Friends	3. 1.1954	Whrecked (rocks)		
Galicia (Armed merchantman)				
Gefion (Norwegian) 5922 tons	12. 6.1917	Mined	Teignmouth (3 miles east)	
1123 tons	25.10.1917	Torpedoed	Teignmouth (10 miles N.E.)Coal	
General Leman (Fishing smack) 459 tons	29. 1.1918	Gunfire		
Gertrude (steamship)	26. 8.1894	Ran aground during fog	Blacknor Point	Iron Pyrities
Georgina (barque) 400 tons	1.1866	Grounded	Kimmeridge (Chapmans Pool)	
Glenmount				
Gloclif 3281 tons	25. 8.1917		Berry Head (9 miles E.N.E.)	
Golden Crape	12.1641	Grounded	Chesil Beach (Wyke Regis)Fruit, Wine, Gold.	
Golden Grove (merchantman)	11.1795	Grounded	Chesil Beach	
Greatham (steamship) 2338 tons	2. 1.1918	Torpedoed	Start Point	Coal
Greleen (steamship) 2869 tons	22. 9.1917	Torpedoed	Berry Head (7 miles N.E.)	Iron Ore
Greta C. (freighter)	7. 9.1974	Sank	Portland	
Hardy (barque)	20. 1.1861	Rocks	Kimmeridge Ledges	Beer, Hay, Mirrors, Coal Beer
Harewood (schooner)	16. 6.1852		Beer	
Harold's Wreck				
Halsewell (East Indiaman) 758 tons	6. 1.1786	Grounded	Kimmeridge	
Hartlepool (steamship) 5500 tons	5. 7.1940	Gunfire	Weymouth Harbour	

NAME	DATE OF SINKING	HOW	POSITION	GENERAL
Hazard HMS (Gun Boat) 1070 tons	17. 2.1894	Collision	Chesil/Portland	
Henrietta (Fishing smack)	21. 2.1812	Grounded	West Bay	
Heroine (barque)	29.12.1852	Rocks	Lyme Regis	
Herzogen (Cecile barque)	25. 4.1936	Wrecked	Salcombe	Wheat, Grain.
Hickory (trawler) 505 tons	22.10.1940	Mined	Portland Bill	
Hildegarde	10.11.1900	Grounded	Kimmeridge	
Himalayer (Former troop ship)	12. 6.1940	Bombed	Portland Harbour	
Hood HMS	1914	Sunk as block ship	Southern Entrance to Portland Harbour	
Hope (Hoop) 350 tons Dutch	16. 1.1749	Grounded	Chesil Beach	Gold Bullion, Jewels.
Hound (Revenue Cruiser)	1836	Foundered	Weymouth Bay	
Hanna	1795	Wrecked	Chesil	
Inisinver (merchantman)	5. 9.1960	Hit submerged object	Portland Bill	
Iris (Swedish brig)	1822	Grounded	Chesil Beach	
Isbjorn 5979 tons				
Isobel (Privateer)	28.12.1600	Foundered	Chesil Beach	
Iolanth	4. 1.1918	Torpedoed	Portland Bill	
James Fennel (Admiralty trawler)	21. 2.1945	Rocks	Portland Bill	Railway Stock
James Egan Lane 7176 tons	21. 2.1945	Torpedoed		
Jane Catherine (Welsh schooner)	23.11.1872	Grounded	Chesil Beach	
Jane Eliza	15. 1.1851	Rocks	Sidmouth (Chit Rocks)	
Jeune Rose (brigantine) French	1. 1.1854	Cargo Shift	Lyme Regis	
Joanah (bark) 200 tons	1707		Weymouth Bay	

NAME	DATE OF SINKING	HOW	POSITION	GENERAL
John (Cargo vessel)	1573	Sand Bar	Exmouth	Salted Fish from Newfoundland
Julia (brigantine) 148 tons	1867	Sand Bar	Exmouth	
Junkers 88 (German WWII aircraft)	1942			
Karina (catamaran)	17. 1.1969	Rocks	Lyme Regis	Chestnuts
Katherine	1702	Grounded	Weymouth Bay	
Kendal Castle (liner) 38859 tons	15. 9.1918	Torpedoed	Berry Head	
Kennet (schooner)	26.10.1870	Grounded	West Bay	Oats
King Charles II (trawler)	30. 3.1970	Leak		
King George (smack)	27. 8.1887	Rocks	Portland (Black Rocks)	Limestone
U-24 (submarine)	10. 1.1904	Collision	Portland (west)	
La Notre Dame de Montaigne	20. 1.1701	Foundered	Weymouth Bay	Timber
Laguiticus de Lille Dieu (Spanish)	1748	Rocks	Lyme Regis (East Cliffs)	Wool
Lancelot (spitsail barge)	27.11.1909	Grounded	Burton Bradstock	
Lanoma (iron barque) 665 tons	8. 3.1888	Grounded	Chesil Beach	Australian Wool
LC(T)A. 2454 Landing Craft	13.10.1944	Swamped by surf	Chesil Beach	
Le Jean Bart (smack, French)	30.11.1838	Grounded	Burton Bradstock	
Le Mercura (French) 500 tons	4. 3.1818	Rocks	Chesil (Chesil Cove)	
Liberty (schooner)	25. 9.1868	Grounded	Kimmeridge	
Lily (pilot boat)	28.10.1927	Holed	Portland Harbour	
Lily (Naval Auxilary)	25.12.1943	Collision	Portland Bill	
Little Belt (smack)	1.1857	Grounded	Chesil Beach	
Lively (sloop)	1824	Carried over Harbour	West Bay	
Lord Duffus	5. 3.1894	Rocks	Portland	

NAME	DATE OF SINKING	HOW	POSITION	GENERAL
Lord Stewart (Armed coaster) 1445 tons	16. 9.1918	Torpedoed		
Louise (Swedish brig)	28.11.1838	Grounded	Chesil (Abbotsbury)	
Louise (brig)	8. 2.1865	Grounded	Seaton	
Louis et Eugenie (French brig)	30.12.1869	Wrecked	West Bay	Wheat
Lumyron (Greek steamer)	15.10.1907	Grounded	Chesil Beach	
Lydia	17. 3.1853	Grounded	Seaton	
M2 (submarine)	26.1.19	Failed to surface	Portland (west)	
Margaeret	2 2.1872	Grounded	Salcombe Mouth	
Madelaine Tristan (schooner)	20. 9.1930	Rocks	Chesil Cove	
Magnet	1829	Foundered	Burton Bradstock	Gin
Maria Louisa	27.10.1838	Grounded	Preston Cliffs	
Marie Elizabeth	25. 2.1874	Grounded on sand bar	Exmouth	
Marie Leocadt (Leocadie)	24. 1.1868	Hit sand bar	West Bay	Coal
Marie Reine (barque) 600 tons	21. 1.1875	Grounded	Chesil Beach	
Mary	1.1817	Wrecked	Lyme Regis	
Mary Elizabeth	1824	Wrecked	Lyme Regis (Church Cliffs)	
Mary Anne (schooner)	28.11.1838	Foundered	Abbotsbury	
Melbury	19.11.1867	Grounded	Exmouth	
Meteor (packet paddle steamer)	23. 2.1830	Rocks	Portland (Ope Cove)	
Minerve (French submarine)	19. 9.1945	Rocks (lost tow)	Portland Bill	
Minnie (schooner from Padstow)	1.12.1882	Bem	Kimmeridge (Berry Head)	
Moon	2.1817	Rocks	Exmouth (Orcombe Point)	

NAME	DATE OF SINKING	HOW	POSITION	GENERAL
Moidart (steamship)	9. 6.1918	Torpedoed	Lyme Regis (7 miles S.W.)	
Morning Star (ketch)	4. 6.1909	Grounded	Kimmeridge	
Myrtledene (steamer) 2500 tons	25. 4.1912	Rocks	Portland (Mutton Cove)	
Newholm	8. 9.19	Mined	Scar Point (1 mile south)	
Nordead (French mud hopper)	12.11.1924	Grounded	Eypes Mouth/West Bay	
Nor (Norwegian steamer)	18. 1.1887	Grounded	Chesil Beach	
Northville 24729 tons	17. 2.1918	Torpedoed	Berry Head (3½ miles S.E.E.)	Coal
Oxahandja (steamer)	8. 6.1910	Rocks	Blacknor Point, Portland	Bridport Grit
Olive (ketch)	11. 1.1895	Holed	West Bay Harbour	
Opha (trawler) 150 tons	7. 1.1976	Grounded	Portland	
Ora Et Labora brig, Norwegian)	13.10.1891	Grounded	Chesil	
Osprey (steamship)	10. 7.1866	Collision	Portland	
P.55 (US submarine)	8.19	Sunk as sonar target	Portland (west)	
Pabla (steamer)				
Panda (schooner)	18. 1.1867	Wrecked	Lyme Regis	
Partia	26.10.1903	Grounded	Chesil Beach	
Patroclus (steamer) 5509 tons	13. 9.1907	Rocks	Blacknor Point (Portland)	
Patria (barque, Norwegian)	26.10.1903	Grounded	West Bay	
Pauline (Brigantine) 130 tons	9. 2.1861	Grounded	West Bay	Corn
Peggy	1762	Rocks	Portland Bill	
Perron (French cable layer) 3312 tons	1. 9.1917	Torpedoed		

56

NAME	DATE OF SINKING	HOW		
Petrorilla (barque, Belgian)	9.12.1856	Grounded	Chesil Beach	
Phoenix (ketch)	22. 2.1923	Holed	Portland Breakwater	
Piedmont				
(military transporter)	18.11.1795	Grounded	Chesil Beach	
Pollux	17.10.1820	Grounded	Chesil Beach	
Pomerian ian				
Preveza (steamer, Greek)	1930	Grounded	Chesil Beach	
Prometheas (schooner)	29.11.1835		Seaton.	
Providence 240 tons	9.1868		Seaton/Sidmouth	
Ranger	26. 4.1 5	Grounded on sand bar	Dawlish Langton	
Record Reign (Q ship) ketch	8. 2.1935	Off course rocks, wrecked	Littleham/Sidmouth	
Reine des Cieux (ketch)	12. 1.1930	Wrecked	Eypes Mouth/West Bay	
Revenue Cruiser	1770	Foundered	Weymouth Bay	
Royal Adelaide				
(Iron built clipper)	11.1872	Grounded	Chesil (Nr. Ferry Bridge)	Rum, Gin, Cotton etc.
Recovery (schooner)	8. 9.1868	Foundered	Seaton	
Reine (French ketch)	5.12.1914	Grounded	Chesil Beach	
Sainte Goymelot		Grounded	Portland Bill	
Sainte Michael				
(ketch, French)	31. 1.1937	Wrecked	Lyme Regis/Charmouth	Timber, Cloth, Sugar.
Sagittario (brig)	21. 1.1840	Grounded	Chesil	Member of Parliament killed
Saladin (balloon)	10.12.1881	Blown out to sea	Lyme Bay	
Salsette				
(steamship) 5842 tons	20. 7.1917	Torpedoed	Portland Bill (15 miles S.W.)	
Samual	8.1812	Grounded	Budleigh Salterton	
Saphire (schooner)	7. 8.1883	Grounded	Chesil	
Sarah	17.12.1885	Wrecked	Lyme Regis	
Scaldis (beam trawler)	1. 1.1974	Foundered	Lyme Bay (Chesil)	
Scud (3 masted schooner)	12. 1.1885	Collision	Teignmouth	China Clay
Sidon (submarine)	16. 6.1955	Exploded	Portland	

57

NAME	DATE OF SINKING	HOW	POSITION	GENERAL
Solebay HMS (6 guns)	1709	Wrecked	Lyme Regis (Black Ven)	
South Coaster	13.12.1943	Grounded	Exmouth	
South of Ireland	25.12.1883	Rocks	Worbarrow Bay Kimmeridge	
Spec (schooner)	8. 1.1867	Wrecked	Lyme Regis	
Speedy	7. 1.1879	Foundered	Chesil (Ferry Bridge)	
Stralsund (square rigged)	12.1872	Grounded	Kimmeridge Bay	
Swallow	1. 3.1832	Wrecked	Burton Bradstock	
T. A. Johnson (Liberty ship)	10.12.1945	Grounded	Egmont Point, Kimmeridge	
Teaser (sailing vessel)	6. 3.1863		Beer	
Tehwija (3 masted schooner)	1907	Grounded	Exmouth	Timber
Thames (steamer)	2. 1.1891	Grounded	Tor Rocks	Tin Ingots
The Fairway (trawler)	2.12.1978	Grounded	Lyme Regis/Seaton	
Thomas (merchantman)	11.1795	Grounded	Chesil Beach	
Thornborough (Privateer)	2. 9.1806	Grounded	Exmouth	
Treveal 5500 tons	9. 1.1920	Grounded	Kimmeridge	
Trois Amis	19. 1.1817	Grounded	West Bay	
Turenne (French trawler)	1913		Portland	
Venus (military transporter)	18.11.1785	Grounded	Chesil Beach	
Verbena (ketch)	22. 7.1903	Rocks	Portland (Blacknor Point)	
Volante	1.1817	Wrecked	Lyme Regis	
Vriendschap (Dutch galliott)	17. 1.1851	Wrecked	Chesil Beach (Nr. The Fleet)	
Vulcan (schooner)	8. 1.1867	Wrecked	Lyme Regis	
Waitara (Iron clad sailing vessel)	22. 6.1883	Collision	Portland Bill	New Zealand vessel
Warrior (brigantine)	7. 1.1882	Beached	Teignmouth	Coal
Welfare	1371	Beached	Kimmeridge	Silk, Gold, Cloth.
William and Anne	12.1836	Foundered	Lyme Regis	